# YES, IT'S TRUE

## BROOK ADAMS

BookPrintingUK
Peterborough
2019

D A

Robertson

# Contents

# Yes, It's True

As I sit here deep in thought my mind is working overtime
and really cries out to tell a story. First of all, I must say
life is made up of chapters, like a book, so, as I reflect, my
hair is snowy white, I'm arthritic, I've had lots of chapters,
so I'll start at chapter one . . .

Once upon a time on a warm, September evening a
baby girl was born, she was named Grace. She had loads
of black hair and cried a lot, noisily. Her mother was in
shock; it was so cold and unfriendly in this big building
called The Workhouse! She didn't really know what was
happening to her as her mother had died when she was
13 years old, aged 53. Her father worked on a farm nearby
which meant the family were so poor, as working on the
farm only being paid with a pig, and they lived in a tied
cottage belonging to the Gentleman farmer.

This 19-year-old lady in labour really didn't want this
baby. There was no sex education in those days, also no
one ever talked about sex, a forbidden word! Her father
wouldn't have talked to his daughter about sex, so Alice
found herself in this situation.

Alice has 6 brothers and 2 sisters. One sister had left
home and was married and the other sister was only 14
years old. Alice had a very hard life, washing and cleaning,

cooking for her family as her mother had died so young. It seems she often went dancing at the village hall, and lo and behold, this baby was being born, a local farmer's son being the culprit. He'd gone off into the Merchant Navy, pushed by his father, when the news of the unwanted baby spread!

Alice's father welcomed the baby home but it was such a disgrace! Alice was sent to Coventry by other members of the family. Life was so different in those days. Families grew all their own vegetables and it was a cold, hard life, not much heating, only the open fire range, cast iron and it had to be polished with black lead polish, logs chopped and milk from goats they owned, or bought from the farmer from the 'big house'!

Shoes were passed down from brother to brother as they grew taller, they grew into tall, stocky, country lads! Their poor mother was so thin and worked so hard, she died aged 53 of pneumonia one wet, cold morning after coming back from market with the pony and trap. So, Alice had to bring the family up when she was so young!

Well, it's 1936, Grace is born! Mumblings in France, discontent, war brewing.

Grace, a new baby, was taken home to the tied cottage, welcomed by her many aunts and uncles. She was pulled around the fields in a wooden apple box when Alice and her sister Ruth picked blackberries. Then, after 2 years of this hard life with the family, father died, so things changed. The family had to move on and leave the cottage. As the brothers were grown up, they went out into the world, one to Guernsey tomato-picking, some joined the Army as war was brewing, Hitler causing havoc in Germany and Poland, very worrying times.

As it happened, after blackberry picking Alice pricked herself with a thorn from a blackberry bush and ended up in hospital, delirious and life changed for Alice and baby Grace.

So my story continues to my second chapter . . .

# Happy Times

When Alice found herself in hospital in Evesham with blood poisoning, very ill, she had no idea her brother was making plans to help her as man of the family now!

Dad had died and made plans for Grace to be adopted, as Alice really couldn't look after her properly – no money or anywhere to live. So, he brought a form for Alice to sign, with a cross, as her wrist and hand was bandaged. She put a cross on this form, signing her baby away – not really aware what she was doing as she was so ill.

So, Mama came into Grace's life and she was taken to Gloucester to live, only 3 years old. She was very undernourished, so thin and had rickets and had to wear callipers to support her weak ankles and legs.

Well, things soon improved, living with Mama. Grace was given goat's milk and Virol, malt and cod liver oil. Oh! it was a nice house, semi-detached, the only 2 houses for miles around, behind tall, iron gates, 2 orchards, stables with goats in, chickens and a black Spaniel called Judy, a lovely brook at the bottom of the orchards, in Longlevens.

The house was new, very well built with a bathroom – unknown in those days! – but unfortunately there wasn't any water connected upstairs so one couldn't use the bathroom, which was sad but a very large kitchen, big, bay windows overlooking the orchards and apple trees.

The kitchen had red tiles on the floor and a pump to pump the water when you needed it, a large front room with fire range with big, bay windows, 3 bedrooms, outside privy with a wooden seat, with a hole for you to sit on. A lovely, well-built, brick house.

Up the lane there was a slaughterhouse and at night one could hear the dogs howling from across the fields, where there was a dog track.

So, time went by. Grace improved. She had a three-wheeler bike which she rode a lot. Her hair grew and she had a bob with a fringe, her hair was jet black and shiny.

One day she was out playing in the orchards when she decided to collect hay for her rabbits.

"Oh!" she said. "This is a lovely clump," went to pick it up and it was a wasp's nest!

She was stung all over and was plastered all over with dolly-blue bag, so she looked blue but it helped the pain from the stings. A lesson not repeated!

Grace had so much fun, now 5 years old, playing 2-ball against a wall, a whip and top made from screw bottle top, coloured with chalk on the top in different patterns, a stick with a shoelace tied on, one wrapped it around the top, spun it, then whipped it, such fun! Also making dens in hedges and playing at house was a favourite game. One spent all day playing these games, as the sun seemed to shine a lot in those days.

Some days Mama used to get Grace up early, 6am, and go across the fields nearby, picking mushrooms, also collecting watercress from a stream nearby – such freedom. Macaroni cheese, crumpets and toast done in front of the fire with a toasting fork, corned beef rissoles, leek and potato soup – everything was so good and Grace grew and was very happy.

She started school at Longlevens Infant School, carrying her gas mask around her neck every day but didn't really know why? being so young.

One day Grace had her tonsils taken out, as lots of children died in those days if you got a lot of sore throats. She remembers sitting on the chaise longue by the window, eating ice cream – lovely!

Then one day an Anderson shelter was built in the garden. Grace didn't understand what was going on, being so young.

Every Sunday she put on her best clothes and went to Sunday School and met other children as she had no friends where she lived – happy times!

But things started to change – dark clouds forming over the country. Lots of American soldiers about who Grace used to go up to and say, "Got any gum, chum?" as other children did.

She used to go across the fields which were covered in cowslips, and look for lengths of tinfoil that had dropped from the sky, from planes, something to do with radar, as Cheltenham wasn't far way with a lot of airmen stationed there, so Grace was told.

Mama talked French most of the time and she had a sister called Desiree and they conversed in French all the time. Grace couldn't remember talking to anyone much but she used her imagination for friends and was very happy.

One sunny, hot day, Grace was going to visit her Auntie Desiree on her three-wheeler bike when, on the way, which was down a lane through fields, miles from anywhere, she went past a camp which had soldiers in it.

Grace was very young, knew no danger and was so innocent. When a man called out to her and said, "Would you like to see some rabbits?" she got off her bike and went with this stranger behind a big building!

The man didn't touch her but asked her to touch him. He undid his trousers but Grace suddenly ran away. When she told her Mama, they went to the police station and the police wanted to go to the camp and identify the man but Grace was too scared. She thought the man would kill her so she wouldn't do it.

It's 1941, Christmas and Grace got up early, excited to see if Father Christmas had been and, to her delight, her stocking had an apple, orange, banana and some nuts in it. Not forgetting food was rationed and everyone had a fawn ration book which only allowed you very little food and fruit, bananas mostly impossible to obtain, so Grace was delighted – a treat!

During the Autumn, Mama picked all the apples in the orchard. Grace helped her then the apples lay on newspaper in the loft to keep. They used to have plates of bread and jam for tea and Grace used to take packed lunches to school made with paste. Cottage cheese was made out of sour milk.

As the time progressed, food was getting short. Of course, Grace didn't worry but Mama had the problem. The winters were so cold, freezing in fact and Grace had to go along Black Lane, as it was named in those days, later called 'Paygrove Lane'. The lane was like a skating rink, so shiny and frozen and she had a job to walk.

As time went by, Grace went to school as usual with her gas mask and when she came home, it was all in darkness. It frightened her, no gas mantles on. Mama not there!

Where was she? She looked in the goat's sheds, no one there! Judy, the Spaniel, had gone also. Being very young she didn't understand but felt very insecure. Mama came home later.

One night, in bed, she couldn't get to sleep for the drone of planes going overhead. A cat howled outside, like they do, ready for a fight with another cat but Grace thought it was a baby crying as it sounded so much like it. She dreamt of witches biting her most nights, maybe fleas being the culprits. She was told that the planes were called the 'invasion', not meaning much to her.

Sometimes Mama and Grace went into Gloucester to Bon Marche, a real treat, not very often though, money getting very short.

Their chickens' necks were pulled and hung on the pump in the kitchen to bleed into a bucket then Mama and Grace plucked them, took all the feathers off the body then roasted for tea.

On day evacuees arrived next door, 2 boys and a girl, sent into the country from London for safety. They always wanted to play doctors and nurses with little Grace always being the patient and she was sworn to secrecy.

Unknown to Grace, a terrible war was being fought in France. Our lovely young men were defeated and stuck on the beaches at Dunkirk waiting for anybody with ships and boats coming from England to come and save them. Then France surrendered. Things were so terrible. Churchill was Prime Minister and in charge of Britain's safety. Hitler and his army getting stronger and threatening our shores.

Our youth, young men, dying in Lancaster Bombers and Spitfires and Hurricanes, doing a wonderful job but so many getting killed and not coming back home – a terrible time.

But Grace grew taller and lanky, long legs and arms. Life carried on as usual at 'Paygrove', the name of the house. Chocolate blancmange being Grace's favourite treat.

On Sundays, after Sunday School, Mama and Grace used to go to climb a hill not far away, Grace thinking she had climbed to the top but when she got to the ridge she always discovered the hill was higher and, though she tried, she never really got to the top as over fields it went higher and higher.

The summers were hot and sunny, baths in the tin bath in the kitchen and watching flies getting stuck to the many sticky fly catchers hanging on the ceiling – brown, sticky lengths of paper catching lots of flies as there were in kitchens at that time.

Trips into Gloucester to the cattle market to see the sheep and cows was another favourite time for Grace – but things were about to change for Grace for ever. Maybe the goats had been sold at market, also the mushrooms they picked sold to make money as times were hard, not much food about.

Before I start the new chapter in Grace's life, I must say she was very lucky growing up. Nothing is perfect but she never had to witness bombing or the terrible lives other children were suffering in London and other big cities. She never had to use her gas mask or use the Anderson shelter which was dark and damp, designed to hold 6 people. They were made of corrugated iron sheets which were bolted together at the top with steel plates at either end. They were half-buried in a hole in the ground and then covered with earth, erected in the garden. Her shelter used to hold a lot of water; it was so very wet but there if one needed it.

In London and cities, houses were being bombed, houses flattened, all buildings ruined, so much suffering, people being killed and hunger through shortage of food. Grace didn't know anything about that.

One day, whilst out playing Mama called Grace.

"Gracie" Gracie! Come in, there's someone to see you!"

Grace came in and saw a lady in RAF uniform there with Mama!

Mama sat her on the side of the sink and wiped her face with a cloth and said, "You are going on a train with this lady."

A stranger! She said she didn't want to go and started crying. It was 1944 and Grace was 8 years old. The lady dragged her to the station and they got on the train, screaming and crying, "I want my Mama!"

Such a terrible experience for one so young! The train was full of American soldiers.

They all said, "Whatever's the matter?" and Grace cried, "I want my Mama!"

So, another chapter starts 'Being A Slave'.

# Being A Slave

Grace couldn't remember much else, by being tired and upset, of the journey but remembers being stood in front of another stranger called 'Alice' but told 'this is your real Mum'! Being only 8 it was so confusing. She also had a sister called Dawn who was 4 years old.

So began a new life in Blackpool, a café downstairs, a dining room and three bedrooms upstairs and a bathroom. Alice, her 'real' mum was married to someone called Antony – Tony for short.

Grace didn't smile much because she felt unhappy and wanted her 'Mama'. She sulked but life changed. She remembers one day, two years later, hearing a baby crying and she had a baby brother called James. The lady in the uniform who took her from her Mama happened to be Alice's sister called Ruth.

From there on, the years passed and Grace was called by neighbour's the 'little mother' as she did everything for her baby brother, pushed him about in his pram, never any rest for Grace. He had Whooping Cough and it was Grace who got up every night to attend him.

As it was a busy transport café, Alice and Tony were always busy in the café from 7am-6pm. She also looked after her sister called Dawn and never had time for playing out and going to school and looking after her brother and sister.

She was so disappointed one Christmas, having to fill stockings for Dawn and James because Grace still believed in Father Christmas! So innocent but all her childhood went from there.

One day Grace felt so unhappy. Life had no fun in it. She saw a bottle marked 'poison' on the hall stand. She took it into the bathroom and felt like drinking some. Of course, she changed her mind but it did happen and she felt so unloved.

She adored her baby brother and sister and used to tell lovely stories, made up, all three hiding under the feather eiderdown. She had a vivid imagination and told wonderful stories. Some happy times.

They went on picnics to a lovely place by a river in Garstang called 'Nicky Nook' but Grace always looking after her brother and sister.

As Tony had an Armstrong Sidley car they often went somewhere on a Sunday, when the café was closed, for a ride, Alice, Grace's mum always having her front window wide open and the three of them nearly being blown away with the wind as her mum couldn't feel it but it was very draughty in the back.

I think I should mention some facts about WWII. The blackout was on till 1944, heavy curtains being used, no light to be shown outside so the German Messerschmitt BF 1093-4 couldn't see light and know where to bomb.

1940. Winston Churchill became Prime Minister. Bomber Command with their Lancaster bombers kept going on sorties with their Merlin engines to bomb German targets. Bomber Command lost 125,000 young men aged between 19-early 20 years. Fine, young men, a third of who joined, were killed. Such a terrible waste of life. Not forgetting our wonderful Spitfires who saved us from terrible destruction.

Also, there were 35,000 Merchant Seamen killed. Maybe Grace's father was killed also by German submarines.

Another wonderful thing that happened – in Operation Dynamo, 338,000 of our lovely young men were rescued from Dunkirk. 900 boats set off from Ramsgate to pick up our men who were abandoned on the shores of Dunkirk.

Now back to life with Grace who, of course, never knew any of this information as she was growing up but, now she was a teenager, she kept hearing about the Atom Bomb. It seemed to cause the world so much worry!

As she mopped the floor of the café dining room and listened to the radio, as she loved music and sang along, she kept hearing about his terrible bomb of destruction.

There was such a shortage of money, she had holes in the soles of her shoes. She used to cut cardboard off the large boxes of flour which was used for baking in the café.

At night the cockroaches used to crunch under her feet. when she looked in the pantry, it seems cockroaches liked flour!

Grace remembers when she was whistling with a penny whistle – a whistle with a hole in the middle – tin, size an inch across. You sucked in and out to make it work. Well, Grace swallowed it! She was terrified! She thought she would die. She dare not tell her mother as she was very frightened of her and what might happen!

Years went by. Grace had such a long way to go to school. If she missed the school bus she had to run over a mile to school, which happened nearly every day as she had to dress James before she had her porridge and James just wanted to play games and wouldn't get dressed and kept running way.

Poor Grace was in detention most nights, also, in the senior school, she never had a uniform (brown skirt, white blouse). Alice, Grace's mum, didn't believe in uniform so Grace stood out in front of classmates every week to explain why she wasn't wearing it. She always said it was being washed!

It was an all-girls school in one half the school and boys the other side of the school. No one would believe Grace hadn't mixed or spoken to any males in her life! She thought they were another specie! Amazing really, she was so shy she couldn't speak to any boys. There were always certain girls who were nice-looking, dressed well, confident, who the boys liked.

Grace used to envy them. She was bullied at school by other girls and one day had a fight with a girl called Marina Smith. They were always asking for money. They used to swap buttons and beads. One never had sweets as sweets were rationed but one could buy Zubes and Victory V which were cough sweets from the local shop. Also, from another shop, for a penny, you could buy a little glass of dandelion and burdock, sarsaparilla and other herbal drinks. It was called 'The Herb Shop'. Alice and Grace used to soak Senna pods every week and drink it, supposed to stop you being constipated.

Grace pushed James in his pushchair everywhere when she wasn't at school and one day, coming down Caunce Street after being to the herb shop, they, James, Dawn and Grace, saw a rocket with flames coming out of its back. To this day neither Grace, or her sister Dawn, know what it was.

Grace used to love cooking at school, sewing she struggled with but made some lovely things such as belts, tea cosies, all with embroidery on them. she had to eat porridge every morning and if she couldn't she had to eat it for her tea. She wasn't allowed to go swimming by her mother but used to go to Cocker Street baths after school and say she was in detention. She loved swimming.

She wasn't allowed to do her homework at home so she sneaked in and did it by lamplight sitting on the bedroom windowsill.

Alice was ever so strict. Grace remembers getting off the school bus one day and Mama was stood there, waiting for her. As her mother Alice had told her not to ever speak to her again ever, she didn't speak. She ran away. Something she regretted for the rest of her life.

Funnily enough, Grace was good at singing and at school was picked for one of the fairies in 'Iolanthe', 'The Pirates of Penzance', in musical festivals, singing also for her team of yellow named St Joan, competing against other teams: green, blue and red.

Any time after school or at school holidays, Grace used to take James and Dawn to Stanley Park to play on the swings and look at the ducks on the lake. It was a lovely park, full of flowers. Unfortunately, on a few occasions by the lake, they were playing and a man would 'expose' himself! Why? Terrible really, as we were so young. Why would they do that? It happened a few times. The police were told and some policewomen in civvies went by the lake to try and catch the culprit but Alice never heard about the outcome.

As Grace grew up in her sheltered world, she later learned that 60 million servicemen died during WWII. It seems President Nixon demanded a bomb to be made to try and end the war so, on August 6th 1945, 'Enola Gay', the plane's name, at 8.15am, dropped a bomb called 'Little Boy', a gigantic atom bomb, on Hiroshima and 70,000 people were killed. Then another plane, named 'Necessary Evil' killed 40,000 people. It's unbelievable but, yes, it did happen!

Then the Japanese surrendered and ended the war. The Japanese soldiers were very cruel individuals and did terrible things to the British prisoners of war, especially the building of The Burma Road.

All this was going on when Grace was growing up, living with Mama and before going up to Blackpool but, believe it or not, Grace knew nothing about it. War is such a terrible thing, loss of lives, unbelievable. It's been stated 70 million military and civilians died during the war.

So, getting back to grace's life as a teenager . . .

One day Grace was fascinated with the hand-drawn milk floats which delivered the milk at the time and she always wanted to try it out – why? She doesn't know but this particular day, midday, she tried it out. It was parked outside the café, the milkman enjoying his lunch. It moved and Grace tried to stop it with her leg which was cut open, a very deep wound. What to do? She says she can't tell her mother so she runs so fast the mile to school, terrified the blood streaming down her leg. The teachers were kind and cleaned it up then the deep wound bandaged up. Another frightening experience in her life. She was about 13 years old at the time.

Life carried on and, on another occasion, Grace had to take James, aged 3 years, to school and sit him at the desk with her. The reason being Alice, her mother, was going to the dentist. Grace was kept off school so many times and the attendance school officer calling at the café! She had to look after James most of the time. They also had a dog called Rex, a lovely dog with brown ears and white body.

Well, it's 1951, the war is over, things still coming back to normal slowly but it was such a busy café, Grace was always busy and, as her school life was ending, a teacher called Mrs Wagstaff said to Grace, "Please don't work for your parents!" but, of course, Grace had no choice. She did seem to cry a lot so teachers suspected life was hard and difficult for her.

Well, she was 15 years old, leaves school and starts hard life in the transport café. She had to peel buckets of apples for apple pies made in the café by the cook, her fingers all stained from the apples, also, in the washhouse, was a potato machine which was used to peel potatoes for the café dinners. It was so cold and damp in the washhouse, Grace suffered from chilblains which were red and itchy on her toes. The backyard and washhouse had to be the whitewashed twice a year.

Grace took an interest in pigeons and kept white, fantailed pigeons in the coalhouse on a shelf above the coal. They bred a lot and the baby pigeons were very ugly and turned out to be lovely white, fantailed pigeons, doves.

Also, later, they had a large chicken run in the backyard with about six hens in it. Grace collected lots of eggs from them. The yard was always hose-piped down each day. A very busy day for our heroine from 7am-10pm.

Lots of things had happened since 1936 when she was born – Second World War, 1936 first TV broadcast, 1953 sweets came off the ration but, as time improved, Grace and Dawn went to ballet lessons and loved acting in shows, singing 'I'll Be Your Sweetheart', etc. Happier times. Grace couldn't stand on the tips of her ballet shoes because of her weak ankles. She would have loved doing tap dancing and singing as she thought she was more interested in that.

One day she was on the promenade in Blackpool and she noticed there was a singing contest on the North Pier called 'The Peter Webster Show'. She entered and sang a lovely song called 'Springtime' and came 2nd, the winner being a more modern girl singing a more modern song.

Another song Grace and Dawn sang in their own shows as 'A – You're Adorable' but her mother, Alice, didn't want her to dance tap as she said it was 'common'. But Grace loved singing and her body was full of rhythm. She did go to singing lessons but didn't keep it up.

Grace really liked Mario Lanza. She saw all his films – 'Midnight Kiss', 'The Great Caruso' with Katherine Grayson and Grace imagined she was Katherine with her long eyelashes and beautiful voice.

In the Summer the family went hop-picking in Hereford to raise money and visited her many cousins.

In 1951, Churchill was voted back in as Prime Minister, such an important and clever Prime Minister during the war so things were hoped to improve.

James started school at the school down the road. As Tony and Alice were busy in the café, he didn't get much attention but he was spoiled and had lots of toys bought for him and got his own way. Grace still busy with him, still going to Stanley Park. He didn't eat much, only egg and chips and porridge still for breakfast.

Nothing changed much, only time flying and Grace and her brother and sister growing up. James really got into tantrums when he couldn't get what he wanted. Grace took him to a store with an escalator and James lay on the floor screaming. He wanted a toy car he'd seen and wanted it. So embarrassing for Grace but he was a lovely little boy, so lovable and clever.

As the memories of war fade, life in general improves but Grace's life doesn't. Alice isn't very maternal and as Tony and herself are very busy in the café, as it's a very busy café from 7am-6pm, busy all the time and it seems the 3 children are in the way. They haven't any time for the children so Grace is kept busy looking after them.

She used to take James and Dawn to the Tatler, a picture house in Blackpool which showed non-stop Walt

Disney films. One could sit watching in the warm all day if one wanted to – such fun!

Also, on Saturday morning, the Regent cinema had Saturday Club for children so, for one shilling and ninepence, one saw children's films. It was always full, children queued up in long lines outside, very well-behaved. Cowboys and Indians being the favourite films – Roy Rogers and Trigger, his horse.

Grace started night school to learn window dressing but that didn't last long because she had to be in by 9pm and one night, she always walked home, and she was talking to a friend which delayed her and when she got home the back door was locked and she was locked out! How scared and frightened she was. She kept knocking on the door and Tony came down and let her in but also beating her on the back of the head which was becoming a frequent event.

She was nagged with everything she did, slapped across the face by Alice every day because Alice was unhappy and frustrated with her life so she took it out on Grace.

Grace was so unhappy. She had no confidence because it seemed whatever she did, Alice nagged her. It seemed to her that Alice never loved or even liked her. The 8 years with Mama lost to Alice and she never bonded or appreciated her. She was just like a little mother to James and Dawn.

Tony and Alice were always arguing, sometimes fighting, which upset the children. Grace had to sweep the stairs with a hand brush, the dust flying up in her face and hair, polish the lino on the bedroom floors then told by Alice she hadn't done it right 'so do it again'! No happiness for Grace.

James was given toys or whatever he wanted, he did well at school and grew tall. As Grace grew up, she was very mentally abused, called 'dopey' by Tony, not given time to eat. As she went upstairs for her lunch Tony said, "Hurry up, granny *(or dopey)*, the RAF will be in in a minute!"

RAF airmen used to come in the café twice a day, stationed at Weeton, a camp not far away. The café was open from 7am-6pm, coalmen from the National Coal Board came in the café for bacon sandwiches, Chorley cake, warm, with butter on, homemade pasties, lovely apple pie, custard tarts, everything homemade and so tasty.

There was Ethel, the cook and Emily, washer-up – no dishwashers in those days! Alice was always in a bad mood and took it out on others.

Grace had to wash up sometimes, washing large saucepans, gravy pans, potato and veg pans in the sink, also was the only waitress serving the dinners in the dining room which was the family's lounge and living room after 6pm. The café sold lovely meals – liver and onions, egg and chips, pasty and chips then apple pie, jam roly-poly all with custard, pints of tea all 2/6d.

So, the dining room was always busy and full, Grace dashing around. All the pans to be washed then at 4pm she had to mop the floor, etc ready for family life. Bacon sandwiches Grace served and made earlier at 10am etc, the bread dipped in bacon fat, plenty of it because a lot of bacon was fried.

One day Alice was in a bad mood so she picked on Grace and said, "Go and get a job!" So off Grace went and managed to get a job in a baby clothes shop. One could change and get a job so easily in the 1950s. Grace came home and was so excited and pleased. For some reason Alice lost her temper and put the hosepipe in the backyard all over her – so cruel! Of course, she wasn't allowed to work anywhere else and being constantly hit over the back of the head.

She wasn't allowed any freedom or to wear modern clothes or shoes. When she was about 15, Tony and Alice bought a house; three bedrooms, lovely house at Carleton outside Blackpool. It had 2 acres of land and a large front garden and drive so the family moved there but Grace had to have more responsibilities and sleep at the café and open it at 7am-6pm, cleaning the showcase and tea urn, make the tea in the morning by putting Twining's tea in a tight or stocking, tying the top then pouring boiling water in the urn which was boiled in the back kitchen. So dangerous carrying the heavy pans full of boiling water to behind the shop counter to put in the tea urn – then it had to brew! Customers waiting outside to come in at 7am.

At one time Tony and Alice bought a lock-up café called 'Nicky Nook' down Dickson Road which was busy with illuminations customers. Grace stayed off school in those days to look after it and service chicken and chips, fish and chips at night in the dining room upstairs. Such a busy life which lasted for a few years.

So, time went by so quickly and the family growing up. Dawn went to a special class to learn to be a hotel receptionist which lasted a while but when she was qualified and given a position at the Queen's Hotel as receptionist, she didn't take it as she wasn't confident enough. She was a pretty, quiet girl.

When Grace was 18 a man from the vegetable firm across the road, a driver and drove a Jenson lorry and brought potatoes from Southampton, took a liking to our heroine Grace and said, "I'm going to marry her one day."

Grace didn't like him much and was so shy and blushed all the time when spoken to.

Tony and Alice were more interested in making money than their children which was sad.

Time goes on and our heroine works hard, no pleasure for Grace. Every night, after mopping the café lino floor, cleaning the showcase on the counter, which was all glass and took ages, she had to empty the tea urn, a very big utensil and important to be kept very clean and polished.

After ironing the tablecloths and different things she had to catch a bus at 8 o'clock to Carleton where Alice, Tony, Dawn and James lived in their big and lovely, well-built house with 2 acres of land, outhouses, 2 garages and a nice, large, front garden.

When she arrived home to deliver the takings of the day no one spoke or said 'thank you', made her a cup of tea or anything. She felt so isolated and unwanted. Whatever the weather, rain pouring, snowing, so ignored and then catch the 10 o'clock bus back to the café to sleep where 2 or 3 lodgers were sleeping and no lock on the bedroom door!

One man was an alcoholic. He was kind to Grace and helped her with her chores after the café had closed. The other man, John Rossal, who worked at the National Coal

Board was young and good-looking but he took no notice or interest in Grace as she was so young.

Grace couldn't understand the indifference, the injustice, the neglect and the monumental lack of love and caring. She had a miserable, tormented childhood. She thought about Alice and couldn't understand how she broke Grace's heart. She was being punished because of her mistakes! To deny maternal love to your own child, an innocent child, was cruel and inhuman.

I suppose she felt she had to explain to her why she couldn't love her but never did because she was an innocent young woman forced to give up her illegitimate child and guilt-ridden thereafter but maybe one should be trying to fathom out why her mother, her mental state and what was the root of her behaviour towards her when she was a child.

It's basically of no consequence because of knowing why she did what she did wouldn't change anything. That's all water under the bridge now and anyway, knowing won't help her now, will it?

When Grace was about 14 years old, she remembers Alice and Tony bought a landau and horse to take holidaymakers along Blackpool promenade. The horse was called Tiny, a large, grey mare. They employed a man to drive the landau and horse and look after it. Trying to make money again but, unfortunately, the driver swindled money out of them by giving Tony extra receipts for food, hay and straw so no money was made but Grace had to go after school and let the horse out of the stable every day for exercise. Well, she was terrified as the horse was so tall and lively, it frightened her to death but she had to do it.

Life carries on and Grace is 19 years old and the man from Crossley & Harrisons, the vegetable firm across the road from the café, called Robbo, started to take more interest in Grace. She hadn't had any boyfriends before in her life but she wasn't very interested in Robbo. He was an older man and had been in the Army for 5 years in Kenya. He kept asking her out for a date but she wasn't interested because she liked Mario Lanza and Richard Todd and she fancified about them, especially Marlon Brando – out of reach, of course, but filled her imagination for romance but he persevered, kept coming around hanging about in the café.

Grace used to hide and say, 'Lock the door, he's here,' but in the end gave in and went out with him. He was so attentive, opened doors for her and treated her nicely and made her feel so important after such an unhappy life that they became a couple, much to Alice's dismay.

It's so strange because she used to encourage Grace to go out with him but she said 'no' but when Grace started going out with Robbo, she didn't like it and kept complaining to Grace about it but it started to bring some joy into her life as they used to go out to Pilling Sands and walk along the river on his day off from work.

Robbo had been out of work for a while when the vegetable firm closed down. He had learned to drive in the Army and he got his PVL licence (Public Vehicle Licence) so he got a job working for the Ribble coach and bus firm as a bus driver. He was 26 years old and really liked Grace who was so young and innocent.

Before all this happened, at Weeton Camp, an air force camp outside Preston near Blackpool, a cousin of Grace's called Thomas was stationed there and came to see the family and visited a lot. Grace had a crush on him and they had one kiss in the backyard of the café and Grace remembers seeing 'stars'!

The airmen who were stationed there used to come in the café for food twice a day, 11am and 3pm, making it very busy for the staff. Lovely bacon sandwiches, pasties, egg custard tarts, Chorley cake with butter on, still warm, apple pie, all homemade by Ethel, the cook. Grace and Tony serving and Emily washing up. It was a busy transport café.

When Grace was about 16 Alice gave her £5 and said, "Get out!" Why? Grace sat upstairs on the bed all day, terrified and shaking. Where was she going to go? And with £5 she wasn't worldly-wise and very innocent, frightened of the outside world and no friends. She cried every day and felt very unhappy.

She heard about the Land Army and thought about running away to join as 80,000 women were working on the land as the men had gone to fight in the war, growing food for the people of Britain as there wasn't any food. The ships trying to bring food to Britain being destroyed by German submarines in the English Channel.

Also, Grace thought about joining the WRENs, hoping to travel and see the world. She did write to the Ministry, received a letter back to say the only job they had was in the laundry. Grace didn't fancy that so nothing changed, still working long hours and hard work at the café.

Down the road, at the side of the café, Laycock Gate, there was an Army barracks, a training place for Territorials and on a Sunday Grace had to open the café, on her own, to feed dinner and food to anyone who wanted it. All the cooking and washing up done by her. Alice and Tony stayed in bed all day on a Sunday for rest.

Grace longed to go to the Tower aquarium in Blackpool to see the fish or upstairs to the zoo they had in the Tower. Most teenagers used to go there on a Sunday afternoon.

At 6 o'clock Alice got up, she couldn't say a kind word or any thanks to Grace for her hard work. Grace had cleared up and cooked braising steak for the family which they had for their dinner every Sunday.

Before the barracks was built up the road it was called Queenstown and, earlier in her life, after school she had to go and sell pasties and sandwiches to the poor people who lived in the little dark houses; pouring rain, wind, whatever, she still had to go and knock on the doors and sell food! That was before the family moved to Carleton and the big house.

When they moved to Carleton, Alice and Tony, still trying to make money, had pigs – Sally and Peggy – which were sired and had lots of little piglets which were sold. The place where the piglets were born was like a maternity ward, all clean, butter muslin put up to divide the pigs. There was one piglet which was the runt of the litter which was fed by hand and grew to be a lovely pet called Lola. She used to run up the drive like a dog and come in the house like a dog. She grew fat and big and had to be sent to market.

There were turkeys to be reared by hand, fattened up for Christmas. Very hard to rear turkeys from chicks as they are frail at first. There were hundreds of chickens in the large greenhouse in the 2 acres of land at the back of the house. Eggs sent to the egg marketing board nearby but such a lot of work for the family. Grace cleaning the pigs out at weekends, pushing a heavy wheelbarrow about, amazing really.

Another thing to remember, earlier, in 1952, when King George died and our Queen Elizabeth was on honeymoon and her father died and she had to come back home and be crowned queen, she had just got married to the Duke of Edinburgh. She was only 26 years old.

Remember, reader, I am reflecting on the life of our heroine Grace. She is now growing up fast, a very unhappy life, restricted of any fun or affection, life seems only to work from 7am to 10pm but we are approaching another chapter of her life so let me continue . . .

When she was 13, she was adopted by Tony so her surname is changed again, not that it seemed a big event in anyone's life. Nothing changed due to this event.

So, life carries on and Grace has grown tall and lanky, no confidence in herself and frightened of the outside world as she has had no experience of it outside the café. No time for friends or fun, only work. She continues to go out with Robbo as he is very fond of her and says he wants to marry her.

One day, a Saturday, Grace worked at the café as usual. She got home to the big house in Carleton and was nagged again by Alice for being late home and was sent to clean the chicken hutches out and feed the pigs. It seemed there was an uncle visiting Alice, her brother and they were going out with Dawn and James to The Pleasure Beach, a large funfair outside Blackpool, famous for its rides and big dipper rides.

Well, something snapped in our heroine – she decided to run away. She had had enough of this unhappy life. As Robbo knew she was being illtreated and very unhappy he kept saying, "Come to my house if you need to."

So somehow, Grace got full of confidence and got her small bag and put her horse ornaments, which she loved, in the bag. It was so dramatic – it was thundering and lightning as she ran with her bag of precious things down the back alley behind the café to catch the bus to Robbo's where he lived in Bispham, outside Blackpool.

There was a cement works at the bottom of the alley where a customer of the café, the owner, worked. Grace remembers he always had a happy, healthy face which he said he put Vaseline on every day! With it being Saturday, most places were closed. She felt like Lorna Doone running away, pouring down, thunder and lightning but it did happen.

Well, Robbo lived with his mother who was in her 70s and he looked after her. Grace was welcomed with open arms but she suffered a bad phase of nervousness due to her being scared. Alice and Tony would come to take her back. As it happened Grace got a job straightaway at the local laundry and started on the Tuesday following running away on Saturday. She got a job as a packer and on her day off at weekends, if Robbo was off, as he was a bus driver, they used to go along the river at Pilling Sands – happy times.

Now Grace's money came in very handy as Robbo was the only one bringing money into the household.

His mum was an invalid, having ulcers on both legs and didn't have any money, only a small pension and she was in constant pain and used to take lots of Codeine tablets which helped the pain but wasn't good for her. She never went out and her skin was yellow and sallow due to no fresh air.

They, Robbo and his mum, were poor really, no cupboards full of food. Grace remembers the first Christmas having a stuffing tart, made with packet stuffing and pastry.

She ran away in the August before her 21st birthday. On her 21st birthday, no cards or cakes but some of her workmates gave her some ear-rings and bits and pieces.

The job of packing was hard, one had to be very fast at packing sheets, pillowcases, shirts, etc. The items had to be sorted first into piles on top of the customers' laundry books and when the items were all there corresponding to the laundry book one could pack them. It was a terrible atmosphere. One wasn't allowed to talk and there were 8 aisles of packers and an overseer who told you off if you weren't quick or talked but Grace stood that for two years. She had got herself a little dog called Rusty which she carried around in her bag on the bus, etc when it was a puppy. They were called a 'black and tan' dog breed.

The year is 1957. Robbo has been in the Army for 5 years in East Africa in Kenya. He loved his time in the Army and now belongs to the Territorial Army which meet on a Sunday. He loved Kenya, Mombasa and would love to return and live there. He's worked at Crossley & Harrisons, the vegetable warehouse since he came home from Kenya. He drove a Jenson lorry which he loved and took a great pride in. He travelled to Southampton docks and picked up potatoes. One day he was on his lorry when the crane above him broke and loads of bags of potatoes descended onto him. It could have been fatal but he wasn't hurt much at all, thank goodness!

Robbo was 29 years old. He was 5ft 8ins, slight build, blue eyes, light brown, fine hair, a very gentle man, not had many girlfriends.

Before he was in the Army he worked on a farm and used to sing to the cows when he milked then. He was a great fan of Frank Sinatra and belonged to the Frank Sinatra Fan Club in America and had all his records. It seems he was late to work quite a few times and used to say to the farmer as his excuse, "I can't get here until I wake up!"

He really was in love with our Grace. She was so shy and didn't know much about men and relationships. She didn't know how babies were conceived; she knew a bit but not about a male's part of it. So innocent!

When she arrived at Robbo's, after running away from the café after working there for 6 years, Robbo's mum Celia really protected Grace from Robbo and told him, "No creeping around at night!"

Grace had her own room and was scared of men in general but she felt safe and happy living there. One thing did worry her and that was in those days one didn't live with a man unless you were married. It was called 'living over the brush', very frowned on in those days so Grace was worried about that, also, in case Alice, her mum, would come around and take her back to the café. It all made her very nervous.

Time flew by. Grace going to work and Robbo, by this time, working for Ribble coach firm. Crossley & Harrisons closed down during the 2 years they were courting. He was out of work for a short while and was very short of money. Grace remembers giving him money, 2/6d for a packet of cigarettes as she felt sorry for him. She believes that's how the relationship started really. They started to go out together and 2 years soon passed.

Now Grace didn't like 'living in sin' so one day Grace said, "We might as well get married if I'm living here," so the Christmas of 1957, Robbo bought her an engagement ring, out of a magazine. It was beautiful, a large Zircon stone on 9-carat gold with platinum shoulders. She was trilled to bits and planned to get married on 15th March 1958 at the Register Office as money was short.

March 15th soon came around and Grace wore a beige suit and had her hair done at a hairdresser's, an unusual event for Grace. No hen party but she did go and stay at Robbo's brother's for the night before the wedding. She remembers crying her eyes out that night because Robbo didn't get in touch and she missed him and couldn't get hold of him so she was so insecure she cried a lot.

Alice and Tony said they weren't coming to the wedding as they were too busy at the café so that hurt Grace very much. James, who was 11, was standing in for them. As it happened a friend at the laundry felt sorry for Grace and decided to put on an after-wedding party and her two daughters dressed as bridesmaids which was really nice on the wedding photos and friends from the laundry attended the wedding.

Grace had a terrible headache, nervous, no sleep

and crying a lot but it was a lovely day on the whole in Bobby's garden where they had the reception then went off on honeymoon to London for a week staying at a hotel that had a ghost that walked round at night – so the story goes!

All new for our couple who loved music, playing on their gramophone their 78s records, especially Frankie Laine 'I Believe', 'Your Eyes Are the Eyes Of A Woman In Love', 'Jezebel' – lovely songs, lovely voice!

A week before the Christmas break, as Grace wasn't seeing her family at all, she bought Christmas presents for everyone and made arrangements to meet Dawn at the Wintergardens where Ted Heath was playing. A wonderful band, wonderful music, everyone dancing the quickstep, foxtrot, etc, everyone happy. Grace and Dawn didn't dance, too nervous as they were not used to going out much. Somehow, they were both shy and nervous, all they knew about men was they only wanted you for one thing – to give you a baby! So, they were frightened of the male species. Dawn said that one man said to her, "Are you a virgin?" Strange!

Well, Grace met this sailor, very good-looking and they walked all the way back to Bispham, a very long way in the early hours. They never kissed or touched but talked a lot and Grace really liked him and didn't want to leave his side. He said he wanted her to come to the station next morning as he was going back to sea. She couldn't get him out of her mind for days. She longed to go to see him off – of course, she couldn't, she had only just got engaged to Robbo but, remember, she had never had any boyfriends or been out with anyone else.

33

# Starting Life With Robbo

## After Leaving Home On Saturday August 6th 1957 And Marriage In March 1958

Grace started work in the Co-op laundry on August 9th 1957. A very hard and tiring packing job as explained earlier in her story but life carried on as a couple and they were very happy. They did lots of nice things.

Robbo worked for Ribble bus firm and Grace used to go for rides on his bus to Morecambe 'lights' twice and had a 1-hour stay on both occasions, had a cuppa and fish and chips at a fish and chip shop, a smashing time! Remember this is before they got married. Another time they went to see 'Hell Drivers' with Patrick McGoohan starring in it at the Odeon picture house.

After 2 months living at Robbo's, one day Grace and Robbo went blackberrying. It was one of the smashing and nicest times Grace had enjoyed in a long time. The sun was beautiful and hot and they walked through fields to a place called 'Skipool'. They didn't pick many blackberries though, as they weren't ripe! Grace was very happy

Then there was Grace's 21st birthday in 1957, mentioned earlier in the story. It rained and rained as usual. Grace stayed in bed as she felt sickly but friends at work bought her ear-rings and a brooch, so nice!

They went blackberrying again to Knottend and half filled their basket in 3 hours then went to Garstang village and had their lunch of spam and chips in a smashing country café. They had a lovely time but were frozen stiff. Grace felt exceptionally happy today.

They caught the bus to Cleveley and saw the film 'Meet Danny Wilson'. Grace was so happy she kept saying to herself, "Oh, my love for him gets worse and worse as time flies by." It's so nice to think of our heroine so very happy and in love – and enjoying life.

So, time flies by, March 15th comes around and, as I've said earlier, they get married at the Register Office and enjoy a wedding party at Bobby's house, a workmate.

So now they are in London, on their honeymoon, at the 'Priors Kitchen'. It was a lovely drive, they stopped at Oxford for fish and chips in a hired car, a brand-new Austin A35 with a heater and wireless. They arrived in Frimley at 10.15pm exhausted and tired after their exciting day.

At the 'Priors Kitchen', their hotel, they had coffee and pork sandwiches in the bedroom then off to single beds then straight to sleep as Grace felt so tired and had a headache. We must remember Grace had never been in a bedroom before with a man on her own. She was terrified. She walked along the corridor of the hotel on her first night of her honeymoon to the bathroom to get undressed and then went straight to bed.

Before they left Blackpool, they had called on Alice in Carleton. She was pleased to see them and gave Grace some Tweed toilet water and Tweed talcum powder. Grace was thrilled with them. They called at the café where Dawn gave Robbo a hug, drank their health and showered them with rice. Tweed was nice to use on her honeymoon. End of a perfect day.

Sunday 16th March: got up 11am after breakfast in bed. They left 'Priors Kitchen' and then to: Farnborough, Aldershot, Blackbush Airport, Royal Military Academy, Sandhurst, London Airport, charged 6/6d for cheese sandwiches and coffee then over Kew Bridge to Strand of the Green where Robbo was born, bless him, Kew Gardens, Buckingham Palace, Trafalgar Square, Piccadilly Circus. Had their supper at the Sandhurst café, lovely too, back at hotel 11.30pm – locked out!!

Every day breakfast in bed at the 'Priors Kitchen', every morning 9am prompt, every day bacon, scrambled egg, boiled egg or Finney haddock, boiled eggs, 2 eggs, fried bread also tea, toast and marmalade. They went somewhere different every day all around London.

Monday 17th March: Got up 11am, had a drink at 'Priors Kitchen', smashing too. Before they left their hotel, they had real fun. Grace laughed all the time at her new husband then off to Southampton, 60 miles away. They saw the liner 'Queen Mary' and took photos then on to Salisbury to 'Stonehenge', Andover, eating out at transport cafés as well as Cowherds Hotel where they had coffee and fried fillet plaice, roast potatoes, peas, tomato juice, fruit sponge and custard – 15/6d for two, very nice. Back to hotel 9pm, they had a nice night in at the hotel.

"He did it tonight. I belong to him only now!" said our heroine but it wasn't easy. Grace was so scared, she cried as it really hurt. She thought she would die, just sat with a towel wrapped round her. Robbo spent all night washing a sheet. The money kept running out on the gas fire and he had to keep putting money in the gas fire. Funny, when you think about it but it's real, it did happen. A very important event for the couple when they had only experienced heavy petting before. Of course, Grace had dreamt and wondered and thought about this important part of her life. The first time is so important to everyone.

When Grace was going out with Robbo, after about a year, she wrote to Clair Rayner, a person you wrote to in the 'Woman's Own' magazine and asked 'am I in love'? as she wasn't sure. The agony aunt couldn't really answer the question!

The honeymoon continued, going to lovely different places. Four more days, they were really enjoying themselves then Saturday they both felt niggly, maybe because, well, they both have to go home and a very long journey before them. Arrived home 10.30. Alice and Tony were in bed. They took the car back; the man was in bed also. Robbo got up Sunday morning 5.25am for work. End of lovely honeymoon.

Well, let's continue with our story . . .

Life got back to routine, Robbo going out to work early, bus driving, Grace at the laundry. They lived at Robbo's mum's rented house, only 16 shillings a week. Sometimes Grace was going to work when Robbo came in. They didn't see much of each other. They had a bedroom, the front one, for their own. Grace kept it lovely, polishing the lino until it really shone. She spent a lot of time in the bedroom.

Robbo bought a lovely, contemporary showcase for their room. What a surprise for Grace when the man delivered it on March 25th. Grace found a 3D viewer under her pillow! Also, they used to leave notes on the bed for each other, so romantic!

Grace got a china bambi and horsehead plate for the walls. Grace listened to music on her record player in her bedroom. She loved Glenn Miller to name but one. They used to go on bus rides into the country on his day off at weekends.

One day they had gone for a bus ride and walk when, sitting on the grass, Robbo got ants in his pants. They were having a picnic and he was opening a tin of herrings in tomato sauce when he spilled it all over his new blue shirt – the tomato juice! What a smell on his shirt too!

Then on August 29th, Grace got a kitten off Alice's cat's litter of kittens, little beauty, a female kitten. She didn't know what to call her. After a few days Grace decided to name her 'Mitzi'.

Alice and Tony bought, as a wedding present, a green wicker ottoman and chair to match. It was lovely, Grace loved it. Things of her own! And she felt so happy.

Robbo put £1 on a new suit. The week before Grace bought him some sandals and 100% wool jumper. Things are looking up for our couple, some money to spend and settling into a way of life and a routine.

Robbo got his new suit. It's a shame to wear it, it's so nice, he looks smashing in it.

In June they walked the Golden Mile, had their tea at

the Victory café ending up at the Imperial picture house. They saw 'From Here To Eternity', smashing film. To bed 12am. Grace said, "End of a lovely weekend with my husband, best one yet!"

From August 22nd to September 5th 1959 they went on holiday to Cornwall with the same car they had hired for their honeymoon. Also, Robbo had bought a wonderful Brownie movie camera. It takes colour pictures too, it cost £18 and a projector. It shows their pictures wonderfully and will last a lifetime, it cost £35. He is so thrilled with it, both lovely, well-made articles. They felt so proud.

They set off 6.30am in the lovely car. It was a lovely morning. They arrived in Worcester 12am. They parked the car at the racecourse then looked for something to eat. The car park attendant told them of a place, 'The Star Hotel'. They went there. Oh! what a high-class place. They felt very uncomfortable. They charged so much also. They bought a film then off to the races where they had a bet on every race but they never won a penny! They spent about £2 on the races, it was very nice too, they enjoyed it very much.

At 4pm they set off again, to Wales this time. They had their tea at a little café at Ledbury and took the first movie of the Malvern Hills and stayed the night at 'Rothesay Hotel' in Abergavenny, their faces burning from the sun at the races. Straight to sleep. They both felt so happy.

The holiday continued, visiting cousins in Evesham, Pershore, taking movies, visiting lovely places: Cheddar Gorge, Lynton, Lynmouth, everywhere. One can't name everywhere, such lovely scenery.

Must mention – whilst crossing the downs a bale

of hay fell off a lorry and nearly fell on the front of the car. The lorry was loaded so high and it didn't look a bit safe and the tree branches were knocking lumps of hay everywhere all over their car. Quite an experience for our couple. Never mind, eh! They had such a lovely week together, looking forward to seeing the films they took made them so happy.

Friday came around. They arrived home 11.15pm Thursday night. Next day Robbo went shopping and Grace washed her hair. He bought another film also 2 records: Duane Eddy 'Yer' and 'Dream Lover'. He bought some fish and chips then they went in the car to pick up Mitzi, the cat. She was pleased to see them. They went for a ride to take Mitzi home and then to the café to see Alice and Tony, along the prom. The illuminations were on so Robbo took lots of film. He really likes his movie camera and is using a lot of film!

They took the car back, much to their regret. They really loved the lovely, hired car. 'End of a perfect holiday in 1959'.

Back to routine now with the most wonderful holiday behind them! (What petrol they used to miles when they started at 1295-2792 miles – 34 gallons bought: they travelled 2000 miles altogether, very good too. Met a lot of very nice people and everywhere they stayed at was very good, good food and beds.)

They kept buying things for their home room; rainbow stiped sheets and pillowcases, cotton, egg cups, etc, etc.

November 11th, Grace went to the doctors and found out she was expecting a baby. She started knitting too (yippee!)

Christmas 1959: Alice gave them a cuckoo clock. By Christmas, Grace had knitted 5 baby garments, 4 jackets, 1 dress, yellow and blue jackets, pink dress and jacket. She finished work at the laundry after the second month. The work, stress, built up, it made her nerves bad. One dinnertime she broke and said out loud, "It's like working in a mental home, not allowed to talk," and the pressure was too much for our heroine so that was that.

# Motherhood

Grace thought she might be pregnant as on the 12th September 1959 she said to Robbo, "Let's throw caution to the wind and instead of stopping at the station, go all the way," a saying, reader, in those days, taking no precautions when making love so Grace thought maybe she could be with child. It proved to be right and as she had been married nearly 2 years she was so happy.

Unfortunately, her appetite increased, feeding two as people used to say in those days. She loved peanut butter and lettuce sandwiches. Her only thought she wanted a healthy baby. Grace started drinking raspberry leaf tea, soaking the leaves every day to stop having stretch marks and help with the birth.

On 21st April 1960, Robbo and Grace went to 'Nursery Land' baby shop and bought a carrycot costing £3/12/6 and a bath and stand, £4/9 – 1 coloured pink, the carrycot was mauve and they ordered their pram and canopy, a turquoise and white Pedigree pram £15/19/6 the pram, the canopy £1/19/11 and a mattress 13/11. Only 6 weeks to go before baby now is due.

On May 30th 1960, at 8.20am Monday morning, Grace gave birth to Constance, 7lb 8oz. She was very fair. Fair hair, eyebrows and eyelashes, a loveable little baby. She was born in Milton Lodge and Grace had to stay in bed for nine days. She also got phlebitis in her legs and had to put black poultice on both legs. She didn't tell the nurses about her veins being red, she thought it was normal.

Everyone is thrilled with the baby, especially Robbo but when she came out of Milton Lodge and took Constance to the baby clinic, she had lost 1lb in weight and she had to go into a sanatorium for about a week. Grace was so upset and kept crying, the nurses saying, "What are you crying for, Grace?" She was worried and frightened for her baby's health but, after a few days in the cottage hospital, she came along fine, her cheeks fattening out. They had put her on National Dry powdered milk, Grace had her on Cow & Gate but it was too rich for the baby.

When Grace visited the baby, the nurse said, "You go and find her and see the difference." Grace couldn't believe the difference. Robbo's mum had said never wake a baby for its feed, the baby will cry when it's hungry. Grace didn't like doing that and felt uneasy about it and so Constance lost weight and was sick. When put on the scales at the clinic to be weighed, nobody told Grace what was happening but rushed the baby into the hospital in an ambulance. Grace cried.

At home Grace bought a lovely candlewick bedspread for their bed, £4/9/11. It looks so nice too. Robbo bought himself another camera, a movie one costing £19.

On Grace's 24th birthday, Robbo bought a camera for her and she has taken some lovely photos of Constance who is now 16 weeks old and coming along fine. She coos and laughs a lot; she is very fair with blue eyes. She has started lifting her head up too. The camera Grace has is a flash camera which can be used indoors so she has taken a lot of photos of her new baby. Tony bought her a lovely glass flower bowl in wine glass and very beautiful.

One weekend Grace and Robbo hired a car and went to Devon for two days house hunting. What a hunt too! They saw 3 places altogether. One cottage was nearly falling down with damp, £500. They were so disappointed. One place was too small with outside toilet, £875. Another place they did like had woodworm of which they didn't know. If it wasn't for a friend, a Mr Townsend who looked over it with a fine toothcomb, bless him. They had 24 hours' stay with the Townsends of who they were very fond of, met on their previous holiday. All dreams shattered.

As time went on friction started to come to Grace and Robbo as Constance was a hungry baby and suffered with gripe, wind, a lot, always having gripe water. She cried a lot at times at night. Grace could have pulled her hair out as she was very tired, broken sleep, Robbo fast asleep and wouldn't get up to feed Constance. He always said, "I've got to go to work, it's your job!" So, a bit of resentment was coming into the relationship. Overtiredness for Grace, etc, also living at his mother's, Celia's, it wasn't perfect with a baby.

Celia, not being well, had the fireplace downstairs so it was hard to dry baby's things so Grace bought a Flatley which dried washing, very popular in the 60s.

In September 1960, they decided to get a mortgage, a 100% mortgage, to buy a house. They picked their house which was being built. They had to wait to see if the corporation would grant them a mortgage on Robbo's wages. They are Fielding's houses which are being built on a new estate, £1,850, terrible price but they wouldn't be able to get one cheaper.

Grace had saved up secretly. £100 she had saved and she said, "If I give you £100 can you get me a house?" so that's how it came about. Then they heard the council had granted them a 100% mortgage so 'hurrah'!

They said the builders have started building, they are up to downstairs windows – good job. Then Robbo paid a deposit of £50 and signed the papers. Grace hoped it would be a start of a better and happier life.

Another resentment was building up as now they had a baby. Robbo, on his day off from work, goes to the Ribble bus station to play poker which really hurt Grace.

As Grace held her lovely daughter, she remembered the experience in Milton Lodge where she was born. She remembered Robbo had to work when the baby was due so he took her around to her mother's, Alice's and Tony's to stay, in case she had to go into Milton Lodge and he wouldn't be there. Anyway, her waters broke so Alice took her in to see a nurse. She said, "It's too early so you must go home until you get pains." So back home she went.

Anyway, her pains did start so, at midnight on the Sunday night, she went back into the maternity hospital. So painful, lots of noise made, so other patients told her next day. Grace sat stiff with her baby in her arms and she dare not move her from arm to arm. Funny when you think about it? Life changed for our couple. Grace was a good mother.

On December 16th Alice bought Constance a nice cot and spring interior mattress.

December 17th Grace was feeding Constance when

she felt something grate against the spoon. Yes, it's Constance's first tooth broken through. Bless her!

As it happens, as Robbo has a movie camera, he starts a film club for people with cameras which is a big hit for men where he works. So, a day out was organised to Rochdale to see 10 best films of 1960. They were quite a big crowd, all laughing and joking and singing. They were a happy crowd so Grace really enjoyed herself.

Christmas was spent at Alice's. Robbo had to go to work at 4pm, "Worst luck," says Grace. She always feels lost without him. But they had a lovely dinner and presents.

Boxing Day they had another nice day around at her mum's. Robbo was off today, thank goodness. They walked around to Alice's which Grace really enjoyed. She said, "I always enjoy the simple things in life with my Robbo, bless him."

They took indoor photos of Constance and the family.

A couple of Robbo's friends, who enjoyed the film club, came around to Grace's house once a week and they went to the pictures sometimes and had a fish and chips tea afterwards. Stan, Robbo's friend, helped with the film club and put on a social at the local pub. They – Stan, Doreen and Grace and Robbo – went to Belle View Zoo with Constance. Lovely days out.

April 27th 1961. They moved into their own house – what a day! It never stopped raining. "It was awful," says our heroine. Also, "Never mind, it's all over now."

During the years they have done nice things and bought nice things but a big event is on August 19th – Constance walked her first steps. She was ??? months old. She had been walking sideways all over the house, bless her. After her first steps forward, she is improving every day! She is such a good baby. She held on to furniture when she learned to walk.

When Stan and Doreen came around to Grace's and Robbo's new home Constance would not go to sleep! Grace spent most of the meeting upstairs rocking the cot and as Grace crept out through the door she would start crying again! Quite frustrating for Grace as she had made lots of nice things to eat, buffet-style.

TRAGEDY. As Grace had left the café, life went on the same each day but Tony had got really depressed. The reason? Outside the café building was going on putting pipes underground! It affected trade at the café and takings were down. Tony was really upset about this as traffic couldn't get near the café to park as the roads were dug up. This went on for months and everyone was telling Tony to cheer up but it didn't help. He couldn't shake it off. He was so worried about the loss of customers and staff to pay, also the big house at Carleton, bills to pay and he was very unhappy.

Well, as it happened, all the family were at Alice's house. It was about 6 o'clock on the 11th February 1962. All the family had eaten and sat around watching the television. Alice said to Tony, "Please could you go and lock the chicken runs up." So off he went but after about half an hour they kept saying, "Where's Tony? He's taking a long time."

They kept waiting and after about an hour Alice went to look for him. He was found in the garage; he had hung himself. The sad thing was he was going to the doctors in the morning to get help for his depression. Everyone was in shock and crying. It was awful. The police were called. A shocking thing to happen!

February 15th Tony was laid to rest in a peaceful cemetery under some trees. Grace hoped he had found the happiness he was looking for.

May 30th came around. Constance was 2 years old. She is a happy little girl, big for her age. She also talks very well too. Everyone remarks about how bright and intelligent she is. A good little girl, so happy. She can feed herself. Grace says she hasn't to feed her now. She is out of nappies; she had been for a few months now and she never has accidents! She had lots of birthday cards which she liked very much.

A lot of things happened after that and things changed. James was about 17. Alice bought him a motorbike which he loved but he was a ton-up boy rider. One day Alice came to pick Grace up to go to Blackburn hospital. James was seriously hurt, broken legs, etc. He had gone over a hedge and landed in a river and Alice wanted Grace to go with her to the hospital. Another shock! They went in a taxi. James's rider suit, his trousers and jacket, had to be cut off him. He had steel rods put in his legs and went to Lancaster for 12 months to a convalescent hospital. It took a long time to recover.

On the day Grace went to see James with Alice she got into trouble with Robbo. He banged his fist on the table saying, "I want you here when I get home." He was really mad.

With the shock of everything Alice sold the house with

the 2 acres of land. She said it holds too many memories and bought a boarding house near the sea.

On June 9th Alice moved into the boarding house. "I do hope everything works out well for her," says Grace.

Dawn moved in with her to help run the place. Grace hopes her sister will be happy. Alice gave Grace a washing machine and a rocking chair because she hasn't room for them in the boarding house. Grace was so grateful for the washing machine as anyone might guess!

After Tony died, Alice was so shocked and upset, she lay about in bed and lost weight. It was a terrible time for all the family.

Time flies by so quickly so now we have Alice starting a new life in her new small hotel. So full of hope for the future. Lots of holidaymakers enjoying their stay at her hotel.

Grace's life is busy looking after Constance, taking her out in the pram and going on the promenade for walks by the sea. When Constance is walking, she keeps going up to prams and saying, "Baby, baby," so it starts Grace thinking she would like another baby so as Constance can have a sister or brother and Grace starts to get really 'broody', crying and saying she wants another baby. Robbo is not as keen as he says he's happy with Constance.

Time goes by and Grace gets her way and in 1963 finds she is pregnant again. She doesn't put much weight on this time and doesn't show she is pregnant very much so it's a surprise for all the family and friends.

So, in November, Grace is in Milton Lodge again, in Fleetwood and gives birth to another baby girl, 6lbs 7oz.

She was a lovely baby, jet black hair, lots of it and the nurse said she looked like a 'Beatle', the musical singers!

She was such a good baby. Constance was so fair and this new baby very dark hair. As people came out of the maternity hospital's nursery they said, "Gosh! I can tell your baby. She looks so like you."

Babies were kept in a nursery in those days, one didn't have the babies with them.

On the 3rd day of her life, November 12th, President Kennedy was shot in his head in the motorcade, sat next to his wife. A terrible thing to happen. Another story in history!

Well, on the 3rd day it seems new mums cry after the birth of a baby – hormones? Robbo had been to see Grace and she was so excited about her new baby and telling Robbo all about her.

He said, "I love Constance," which, of course, we all do but it started Grace to cry when he left and other mothers in the ward were saying, "It's nothing to do with us, President Kennedy getting shot. Why is she crying?" They thought Grace was crying about that.

The baby was without a name for about a week as Robbo and Grace couldn't agree on a name. In the end she was named Alison. She was such a good, quiet baby. She sucked her thumb and came on so quickly with having such a happy and lively sister.

When she sat up, months later, she sat in her pram, watching Constance play. So quiet, lots of dark hair, Grace always knitting for her two little girls. She loved making cardigans and jumpers with fair isle on them. The knitting needles clicking away every night in front of the telly. Fortunately, they lived near the seafront so went on the promenade most days.

Now, 6 months before Alison was born, Celia, Robbo's mum had a fall at her other son's where she had gone for a few weeks to stay, for a change of scenery. She ended up in hospital as she had broken her hip. Grace used to ride pillion on James's Norton motorbike with Robbo when she was 8 months pregnant! She loved riding on the back of the motorbike visiting Celia. Robbo used to borrow the motorbike sometimes as the hospital for elderly people was so far away in the country.

Well, the day she was due to come home she had another fall and pneumonia set in and she died aged 76, so that was so upsetting but meant another room for Alison as it was only a 3-bedroomed house they bad.

It's funny how fate works thought Grace as having 2 daughters and it being a 3-bedroomed house, a room each for the girls when they got older. It's very sad how fate had played a hand.

Life carries on, both girls are walking and talking, getting bigger. As their home has a 109-foot garden, Grace is kept busy mowing the lawn, growing rose trees, blackcurrant and gooseberry bushes, life is rosy. Constance is 5 now and starting school in March. Grace remembers how busy she was taking Constance back and forwards from school because in the first years they can't stay for dinners so she takes her at 8.30 to walk to school and picks her up at dinnertime then picks her up 3.30pm. She remembers hanging washing on the line and when she got home it was stiff, frozen, jumpers, etc, in March too. As Robbo works shifts, he isn't there much so Grace is very busy with family life and nearly 30 years old.

About 2 years ago, before Alison was born, another sad thing happened to the family. As I said before, Alice sold her lovely big house of 2 acres, paid off debts and bought herself a small hotel by Derby Baths. The hotel was busy, everything going well when Alice's health deteriorates.

Now, she doesn't tell anyone but she is coughing up blood and when she bends down fluid comes out of her lungs and she gets seriously ill and taken into a TB hospital. The hotel is closed down by the health regulators, tuberculosis is so contagious. No way can holidaymakers stay in this hotel.

Dawn has to sort everything out and, earlier in the year, a young man was employed by Alice to help in the hotel. As it happens, Dawn and this young man called Tim, get to like each other and fall in love.

While Alice is in hospital, they want to get married. Alice doesn't like the idea. She thinks Dawn could do better for herself so Grace does all that is required for a register office wedding. Grace does all the baking and sorts all the requirements out for her sister. So, they got married.

The hotel's sold as it was closed down. Consumption must have been living dormant in Alice. The shock of Tony's death brought it on, strange, after all, her life in the café she was so scared of TB and scalded all her cups and cutlery she used as she was so afraid of the disease.

Unfortunately, with Alice being ill with consumption, all the family who had been in her company had to be X-rayed. Constance had a shadow on her lungs, Dawn had a hole in her lung. Grace didn't have an X-ray, she wasn't asked for by the consultant in charge of the case.

Constance had to take a large pink tablet every day but unfortunately she couldn't swallow such a large tablet and Grace used to break the tablet up but Constance couldn't keep them down but as she was a healthy 3-year-old she got better on her own as Grace knew she hadn't had much help from the tablets as she couldn't take them. She was so worried.

Time flew by. Alice was in the sanatorium for 12 months. It was such a long time and Alice was getting restless to come out of the hospital. She asked if she could go home as her daughter, Grace, was expecting her baby anytime. She was told, "No, you can't!"

She was annoyed about that and wanted to be there for her second granddaughter's birth. She never did like being told what to do, etc so she signed herself out of the hospital. Her consultant was good to her and found her a flat by the sea. Of course, no one could visit her as she was still contagious which really upset her. Grace couldn't take baby Alison and Constance anywhere near her. Everything was so sad and serious. Alice had never been on her own before. She was so depressed and upset.

Years fly by, life's routine for our family. Dawn had given birth to a baby girl in 1963 so there are 3 young, little girls full of life and energy. She, Dawn's and Tim's little girl, is called Beth. She couldn't visit her grandma either but as I said, time has gone by and, believe it or not, Alice really improved. It was the best thing she did to leave the sanatorium as they were so drugged up in hospital. I think she wouldn't have improved if she had stayed in.

She had met a man she had known for years and bought a house, was very happy and planning to get married.

Constance and Alison are doing well at school and growing fast. Robbo is about 39 years old and bought his first car, a banger, only cost £50. It needed a new door but everyone was so pleased and excited. It was a Morris Minor car.

Now, Grace was getting restless and needing more money so she gets a job in a dry cleaner near home. As the girls are much older now and at school all day, money is needed. It's hard work in a hot environment but she worked there for 7 years!

Also a few more cars bought – Vauxhall being Robbo's favourite, also a Hillman Imp. Robbo changes his job as a bus driver and goes on long distance driving so the family see less of him as he's away a week at a time. Grace is very upset at first but gets used to it after a while.

Alice gets married at the Register Office, a happy affair. Grace puts all her energy into being a good mother and making the girls happy. They have lovely birthdays, loads of jelly and ice-cream, cakes, little sandwiches and a cake with candles on it. Grace is still knitting and makes the girls' dresses by hand, both the same with ribbons to match. They look like twins.

Now we must not forget the two little girls' pets. First there was Mitzi which Grace had for about 12 years but her kidneys collapsed so she had to be put to sleep which really upset Grace so Grace got two kittens from a 'cat woman', a lady who saves lost cats. Constance has a male cat which she calls Simon and Alison has a black female kitten she calls Sheba. Simon was a tortoiseshell breed, both lovely, cuddly pets. Cats are more suitable for a family as Grace goes to work and cats can be left and they bring such fun and happiness with them. Grace had Sheba spayed and Simon neutered and they grew into lovely cats.

Now, one day, a funny thing happened. Sheba, the lovely black cat went missing. It seems when Grace went to work, she had found a cosy and warm place to go, another home in which a little old lady spoiled her, giving her Carnation milk and titbits and spoiling her. The little lady said 'God had sent her Sheba' as her cat had got killed on the main road. Whenever Sheba came home to the family house she would come around and say, "Where's my cat?" much to our dismay. She was our cat!

In the end she stayed with the lady and one day Simon got killed on the main road but it was years later in my story.

The work at the dry cleaners was hot and busy but through working there, Grace was introduced to rambling, fell-walking. Her boss used to go every fortnight, walking in the Lake District. Grace was interested and her boss said she could join the walking club.

So, another chapter starts . . .

On a Sunday, once a fortnight, she got up early and she took Alison and they caught the coach into town at 8.30am. There were three parties, A, B and C. Grace used to go on B. They walked about 6 or 7 miles. A used to be for the strong and fast walkers and C slower and older members who walked at a slower pace and only a few miles.

They all met up at lunchtime and sat down for an hour and ate their packed lunches. At about 5 or 6pm, the walks ended and the coach was waiting for the ramblers who got changed and then called at a café for tea, all booked as, on the way to the Lake District, they sent a board around the coach and you chose your menu you wanted so the café knew what you had booked so it was ready for you. Lovely!

We also had a pub stop where you could chill out and mix with other members. The busiest time was in the Winter. Believe it or not, the coach was always full.

We climbed up the 'Cat Bells, Scarfell Pike, Helvellyn. We always had a member who was the leader, a strong walker, who knew his way and was willing to lead. So many miles were covered and lots of fun and something to look forward to. Sometimes it was really hard going up the mountains and when you got to the top, you couldn't see anything due to mist, soaked through in your waterproofs. It does rain a lot in the Lake District but it is a beautiful, lovely place. Coming down off the mountain was hard work on your knees and it only cost £2 a day, so worthwhile to get out – 'a rule of ten' was when you went in the bushes to spend a penny. Certainly, a new hobby for Grace and Alison.

About twice a year the club held a barn dance where the members danced the Gay Gordons and the Valetta, a lot of fun for all. Also, during the Winter months the snow was so deep on the fells it came up to the knees. It was hard work walking in deep snow and it slowed you down.

Once, during the Summer months, some members went to Llanberis where we climbed up Snowdon, walking up the 'pig track'. Hard work but one felt so good after what you had achieved, walking and climbing up into the clouds. Wonderful. This was done on three different occasions, a wonderful achievement. Coming down off the mountain took time. One had to be so careful not to slip, etc. A good day's hiking and going in the café at the foot of Snowdon for a hot drink and sandwich, which tasted so good, finished off the day's climb.

Grace slept well after these days out. When she arrived home about 9.30-10pm routine started all over again. Grace felt hurt that Robbo couldn't, and didn't want to, join in any of these activities. He was so used to going up and down the motorway 6 days a week.

At the back of the dry cleaners is a laundry so Grace worked there a lot. They were always short of staff. She worked on the large calendar which dried and ironed the sheets and folded them.

4 ladies worked on the calendar, two putting the sheets in the rollers, one had to do it properly and get the hems straight and together, two receiving them through the 4 large rollers and pile them up. Sometimes the folder didn't work properly so the sheets had to be folded by hand, a hot job. Large tablecloths for banquets that came from the hotels were done the same way on another calendar.

Grace was so good at folding these very large tablecloths that she had to train new staff but her main job was working on the small calendar pressing and folding pillowcases. It never folded them right, the machine was always going wrong. The pillowcases had to be folded by hand which put Grace behind with her work and very frustrating.

She was near home and Alison used to ring up sometimes and say, "Can I have an ice-cream from the ice-cream man?"

This job lasted from 1971-1978 when the firm went into liquidation and everyone was finished off and the building was closed down and emptied, much to everyone's dismay. End of 7 years' hard work.

"What to do next?" says Grace. There's no work about nearby and she couldn't work too far from home as Robbo worked away all week. Thinking back over the years, Grace used to see Tom, the manager, standing all day, untying knots in aprons belonging to chefs, etc. They had been washed in the large washhouse and had to be tied up during washing or they would tangle up all the washing. As she was thinking Tom always looked under stress, keeping everything going, speed was important in a laundry.

Grace liked Tom, he was a kind man and was nice to Grace. She had a little crush on him, secret of course but kindness goes a long way when one hadn't had much kindness in her life. She worked hard and always did her best. Now she finds herself out of work. She was thinking one day how ironic it was that she ended up working in two laundries!

After when she was a teenager, she applied to the WRENs for a job and they only had a vacancy in the laundry department. She turned it down because she didn't fancy working in a laundry! She wonders how her life would have turned out if she had accepted it? One will never know!

Life carries on and in 1978, Grace has her first holiday. She has a friend called Mary who says, "Why don't we go on holiday together? You take your 2 girls; I'll take my 2 boys. You don't go anywhere."

So, it was all arranged. They went to the Isle of Elba, a little island below Italy, £176 for two weeks for the three of them. The two girls and herself for two weeks. It was such an adventure for our two families, different food and people.

Grace noticed they didn't look after their animals. She was shocked. Cats bred on the island on roundabouts and there were a lot of kittens about – sad.

One day on holiday they all wanted to go to Florence on the mainland. They had to get the ferry. Grace got seasick and felt awful. The smell of diesel on the ferry boat made her feel worse.

She wanted to see Michelangelo's work and his statue of David. They went in the museum. It was so thrilling and wonderful, all his other statues, so perfect.

They walked around Florence and Grace felt better and wished she could find a café that sold beans on toast, all the smell of the spices made her feel sick but it was a lovely first time on a plane and first holiday abroad which she enjoyed so much and got very adventurous, wanting to see other countries and their ways of life and cultures.

But first of all, she had to find a job – not easy. Her age was against her and she didn't have much experience for other jobs. After a few months she got a job at Bollin House, a catalogue firm trying to get households to start their catalogues.

Grace was really good at her job because of her friendly nature. Going from door to door in the pouring rain, knocking on doors made people feel sorry for her so ordered £5 worth of goods to start a catalogue. She got a lot of agents. The firm was really pleased with her and when she wanted to leave after 6 months' work, they tried to stop her and didn't pick their catalogues up for a long time from her house.

Dawn, her sister, looked after the girls if needed but mostly the working hours were during school hours.

When the girls were young, desperate for more money, school uniforms, shoes, basic things, Grace found a job for one day a week. She was always looking for a job and going to the Job Centre on her bike. She really loved her bike.

The job she saw in the paper entailed delivering a local free paper to everyone, put through their letterboxes. The papers were delivered on a Thursday night in bales from the firm. She had 2000 to deliver on Friday and she received £20.

You carry a bag around your neck, take as many as you can carry and you have a large area to cover all in one day. So, Grace walked very quickly and always delivered them all, not missing a house. The free paper was very well liked and popular. If someone never received their paper, they would ring up the firm and complain. One must close gates and not jump over walls. She delivered these papers for a long time, the £20 was very useful.

The problem was the weight of carrying all these papers, so heavy and time wasted having to keep going back home to fill up your bag again. Trolleys, shopping ones, were not invented then, one would have been so useful for our Grace.

One weekend they went to Pembrook in 1945. It was important for the RAF as planes took off from there defending the ships in the Atlantic which were being destroyed by German submarines. Such a place of interest as the planes flew from Pembrook docks. Grace was interested in the aircraft and the war years. It seems no food could get through to England because of the German submarines sinking our boats. A terrible time. Never forgotten.

Now, as our girls are growing taller and have busy lives, they only see their dad at weekends where we all sit together and eat, watch TV and at 9pm every Saturday night have some chocolate, enjoyed by all.

Robbo took his guitar everywhere with him. He was self-taught and loved it. He used to have a friend around, when he could, to play his guitar, an acoustic one, like Robbo's. They smoked a lot, as most men did in that time and never seemed to be without a cigarette. Robbo rolled his own with tobacco, a very important part of his life. Also, he had a Pentax camera and, on the road, he took photos of planes and fields of hay, whatever took his fancy.

In his youth, Grace remembers how his mother cut the top off his boiled eggs in case he burned his fingers! He hadn't had many girlfriends so didn't know much about women. Men took their wives for granted, didn't think they needed taking out or things like that. Grace liked family life but she, herself, hadn't had much experience with men. The girls were her life.

The aftershave he liked was 'Old Spice'. He wasn't bothered about dressing up but Grace loved clothes. They didn't spend much time together due to work. When he was away every night, he always rang Grace up and she looked forward to his phone calls. Sad life really.

Grace and Robbo loved music and were always buying singles when they came out, especially The Beatles, The Rolling Stones, The Eagles and Duane Eddy. If Grace had had a baby boy, he would have called him Duane.

He worked very hard, having to cover all his loads on his lorry with tarpaulin, even in pouring rain and he never stayed off work even when he wasn't well. His brother was also a lorry driver and lived the same type of life, both working on large container lorries which held two large containers. A big responsibility. The drivers of the large lorries were like a happy family and used to meet in motorway cafés and talk lorry talk and eat and drink, not the healthiest food – also smoking.

Years are flying by and, for our family, it really is a routine life. They had lovely Christmases, looked forward to by all. Grace did all the shopping, food, presents, etc. The girls helped her dress the Christmas tree with baubles and tinsel, a happy time.

On Christmas Eve all presents wrapped and put under the tree, the girls went to bed singing 'Christmas Eve is here' as they climb the stairs, nodding sleepy heads and into their comfy beds, off to sleep. Hey ho! Then Grace would fill stockings with pens, colouring pencils, sweets, pencil cases, also leaving a mince pie and a drink of port for Father Christmas.

Everyone was up early. Grace cleaned her front step with Cardinal polish then made grapefruit slices, tinned, lovely, then egg, bacon, sausage, fried bread, toast and marmalade. All tasted lovely. Fruit juice.

Opened their presents then dinner, sometimes turkey, sometimes duck, tomato soup to start first, finish with Christmas Pudding, custard. All lovely. Listen to the Queen's speech at 3pm, eat chocolates and fruit, sit down, rest then 7pm turkey sandwiches, sausage rolls, brown sauce, homemade mince pies then, if one could eat more, cut the homemade Christmas cake.

Then eat it all over again on Boxing Day but a more relaxed day, having pork and crackling instead of turkey. A lovely time but lots of washing up, no washing machines in those days. Pulling crackers was such fun too. A lovely time for the family – lots of chocolates eaten in the evening.

Also New Year's Eve was spent together playing records, lovely meal on New Year's Day. Some coal was put outside front door and the first person through the door brought in the New Year, also good luck for the household. Coal fires were the only form of heating in 1950-1960-1970. Coal delivered by a coalman, a man with a lorry. He was covered in coal dust, carrying on his back heavy bags of coal, one or two, whichever you could afford, as it wasn't cheap.

Rag & Bone man came every week with a horse and

cart shouting loud, "Rag and bone," wanting anything one wanted to throw away.

Remember Grace bought her first bike for £1 from a rag & bone man. He had made the bicycle out of different part of thrown-out bikes. He charged her £1 and she loved her bike.

After the job with the papers delivering, Grace got a job in a shoe shop which really frightened her as one had to go into the back room and look for the other shoe the customer had chosen and was sitting and waiting. Sometimes it took ages to find the shoe she was looking for, a very stressful job but one did improve with experience.

Now one day, Grace saw an advert in the paper for a weekend in Jersey. As it wasn't too dear, she booked for the four of them to fly from Squires Gate airport, a small airport on the outskirts of the town.

Well, Robbo and the family enjoyed it so much. The hotel was lovely and the beach in front of the hotel, they all fell in love with Jersey. Robbo, who never wanted to go anywhere as he was away from home so much, fell in love with the island very much. They swam in the sea and sunbathed, hired a car and went around the island and the time went too quickly.

Saint Brelades Bay, where the hotel they stayed at was situated, was the hottest part of the island so one had to be careful they didn't get sunburned.

Constance suffered from prickly heat as she was so fair-skinned, a very itchy rash came out on her arms and chest. She had to be careful. They went to Jersey a couple of times, staying a week and going to a show at night which had very good artistes, dancers, a real treat.

They raced each other on the sands and one day Grace went into the sea to swim as she liked swimming in the sea. Robbo said, "Don't go too far out!"

Well, Grace felt safe and did go deeper into the sea but got caught in the current. It was so frightening. It felt the sea was dragging her further out. It took all Grace's strength and energy to pull herself out to the shore. It was really dangerous and really frightened her.

When the girls were younger, they went to dancing class, ballet and tap and were on the stage at the Wintergardens a few times in pantomimes, lovely costumes and fun. Time does fly past quickly.

Constance is 17 now and has decided she wants to be a nurse, so when she left school, she got herself a job in a nursing home in St Anne's to get some experience.

Well, the day she leaves home for the first time it's snowing and Grace takes her to the bus stop. They had to walk a little way. When they opened the front door, the snow had drifted so deep! Constance isn't tall, 5ft, the snow was so deep. Grace really missed Constance, leaving home for the first time.

Grace managed to get a job selling jewellery in Blackpool in a big department store on a concession counter for a man who made his own jewellery and had been in the store for many years. With her friendly manner she sold lots of ear-rings and necklets. She worked for this gentleman for 4 years. The store was Binns, a part of House of Frazer group. Grace had to set ear-rings out on cotton wool in pairs to display them, changing the cotton wool quite a lot to keep it clean, standing all day, not allowed to sit down or leave the counter unattended. She worked from 9am to 5.30, an hour for dinner. She used to have an apple and a yoghurt in the staff canteen for lunch then go to Marks & Spencer's to get something for tea, leave the store 6pm, catch the bus home, a half an hour journey or more. Rupert, the white cat they had, with blue eyes, would be sat on the front step waiting for her.

The girls were growing up. Constance living away, Alison let herself in, she used to dust for Grace and do some shopping. Very busy life for our family.

Well, what was Robbo doing all this time? As life was routine for the family, Grace thought he was acting strange. He never paid her any attention, was always down the road staying at the same drivers' digs near Birmingham. It was a sad time for Grace as she felt unloved and no attention paid to her but the girls kept her going.

One night she saw Robbo's folder on the table. He had gone to bed. He kept his driving notes in the folder. She saw a slip of paper with notes on it! Questions, asking questions as Grace used to write to say on the phone.

One question was 'why don't you like me singing and playing the guitar to you?' among other questions. Grace flew upstairs and asked him about the notes. He denied everything but life will change for our Grace.

Another chapter starting: 'Lots Of Tears' . . .

# Lots Of Tears

Lots of things have happened in the family's life. It should have been mentioned earlier in the story.

James got married when the girls were young. He had a big wedding at a lovely church. The reception held at the Savoy Hotel. The three girls, Constance, Alison and Beth were bridesmaids. Grace had their hair styled at a hairdresser's but it was a damp, windy day. They looked lovely but their hair dropped, much to Grace's dismay. A lovely time shared by all.

Also, Alice had got married to John and had moved down south to the South Downs, a place called Steyning, a lovely place. They are very happy and have three dogs, a chow and two collies. They go on the Downs every day to take the dogs out. So, everyone is living their lives.

After many years, Alice and John want to come back to Blackpool to be near family, mainly James, so she asks James to find her a house. He finds one and Alice, John and the dogs move back to Blackpool.

Grace always wanted Alice to come around to see her and have a cuppa and some homemade cake. It never happened. Alice never went anywhere much, so Grace went around to see her a lot with the girls but time was short as work and family life kept her busy.

So, life carries on for everyone. Grace's daughters are

teenagers, they shop at the Co-op around the corner and Cleveley nearby. Grace feels hurt thinking Robbo has feelings for someone else but thinks, 'no, I'm imagining it'.

2 years pass; Grace working at Binns, Constance training to be a nurse at a hospital in Preston. Alison is now working as a secretary for an estate agent. Everyone busy.

One Saturday afternoon Robbo comes home as usual and says he's leaving and in love with someone else.

Grace is shocked, gets on her bike and, crying, goes around to Alice's, riding through the country lanes as fast as she can. She always thought they were a lovely family of four, striving to exist against the world, very secure. What a shock!

Alice says to John, "Have we some brandy?" which they have and gives Grace a glass. She is so upset, crying so loudly.

Time carries on, routine prevails. Robbo still comes home every weekend. He sits and watches television and acting as he always did, not speaking much.

Grace always asks, "Are you still leaving?"

He says, "Yes!" in a drawn-out way.

Grace remembers, about year before this happened, she booked a holiday to Menorca. They stayed in a lovely hotel in Mahon. It had a lovely view of the bay. Robbo acted so cold and indifferent. Grace couldn't understand his behaviour. Strange? Which made her act hurt and offhand. She couldn't believe it.

Life goes on. Grace is so upset about her life, so insecure, crying a lot. Of course, Robbo is only home on a Saturday night, not interested in making love or being civil, acting so out of character and it upset and hurt the family, causing an atmosphere. This went on for ages.

One day, when Grace had been out rambling, her mind full of this problem at home, she went home with her mind made up.

She said to Robbo, "Are you still going?" and he said his usual slow, "Yes."

Grace flew upstairs and got his clothes and said, "Go then, now!" and threw his clothes over the banisters, downstairs and said, "Go then," and he did.

Of course, Grace suffered emotionally. She had a breakdown; she lost the use in her legs for a while and had to go down the stairs on her bottom. A lot of crying and loneliness. She thought he would come home as usual on Saturday as it was their 30th wedding anniversary. Of course, he didn't. It was a terrible time for poor Grace.

After a few lonely, unhappy months, Grace put in for a divorce. Robbo didn't want her to but as she had been betrayed and hurt, she went through with it.

As Grace had a barrister on her side, she was given the house because of her age and working days, not able to earn good money as fate had a hand in her life,

Grace was singing in a show, 'My Fair Lady' which was on at the Grand Theatre in Blackpool. So, the show took over her life and kept her very busy so that helped her through the divorce period. She kept receiving letters from Robbo and his new love to sell the house and buy a house in Fleetwood, which Grace ignored but it hurt so much.

She got a job at a big superstore in the town centre on the jewellery counter again. Another chapter starting in our heroine's life, some fun and happiness for a while anyway!

Alison had met a young man at night school and was busy with her life, working as a secretary and going out with her boyfriend.

Two years passed, lonely nights waiting a bus at night at 9pm as she worked until 9pm. Long hours in Winter, very cold and dark, waiting for a bus and when she got home, she could hear silence. A very sad time.

Well, after working on this jewellery counter, there's a very handsome man working in the store and he catches Grace's eye. As he passed the counter he used to say, "Hello, sunshine," which thrilled our Grace as she had not had anyone notice her for years.

As time went by, he stood in front of the counter and they got friendly. As he passed at dinnertime he said, "I'm going for a liquid lunch," which Grace didn't know what he meant.

One day he asked her if she would like to join him. Gosh! "He was so handsome and beautiful," said Grace so they went for lunch nearly every day and Grace fell in love. She was so happy. He was called Stephen and used to buy her lunch for her in a local pub.

One day, after some nights out to a local Indian restaurant, Stephen turned up at her home with his hand behind him. He had bought her a plant for a surprise. So, after a while, he moved in. The family loved him as he was such a happy person and lightened everyone's spirits.

She loved being in the show 'My Fair Lady'. The show was on for a week, a matinee on Saturday. With two shows on the Saturday, the adrenalin was high with all the dancing and singing and it was a great success. Everything was looking up.

The Grand Theatre is a lovely Victorian theatre, very special to Blackpool. The lovely costumes, the cast, wear, makeup and happy company is so important to Grace and the music is beautiful. It helped her through a bad time in her life, going through her divorce and all the stress. As I said before, it was something to concentrate on and take her mind off unhappy things.

Another important chapter is taking place lasting ten years. Some happy times and some stressful with Stephen.

He got finished off at the supermarket where he worked as head for a team of cleaners. When a woman is in love and in a new relationship, she will be blind to faults in her new love and put up with lots of things she shouldn't have to.

He also was very good-looking. Grace was besotted and loved being with Stephen but she was a very insecure person and suffered a lot of stress due to this condition. After being hurt by a man so much it never leaves you and you don't see your own worth.

Life settled down to routine. Grace and Stephen were very short of money and tried lots of different things to make money. Stephen got a job at a big supermarket collecting shopping trolleys and after that, realised he had a carpet cleaner, industrial, from his earlier cleaning job so they set out cleaning carpets and settees, stair carpets, etc. It was amazing how busy they were. Hard work but it paid the bills. Grace cleaned stair carpet and Stephen carpets and furniture. They did a good job at cleaning so, by word of mouth, the jobs came in. Being busy using the carpet cleaner lasted about 2 years.

Another job they did was going around on one day, Friday, delivering the free paper in rain, wind, whatever the weather, jumping over walls, Stephen doing one side of the road and Grace the other. They had to move fast as all, thousands of papers, had to be delivered in one day on a Friday. That brought in £20 so needed by the couple but hard work again.

On a Saturday night sometimes, they went to a working men's club and really enjoyed themselves. They danced together and Grace dressed up in her lovely clothes and looked beautiful. She was happy and had never been out before for a night out so she shone and smiled a lot and after a while were noticed by other club members and became club members themselves.

Before meeting Stephen, Alison had a lovely wedding and had married her boyfriend Jack.

Constance had moved to the Channel Isles working as a nurse. Robbo and Grace encouraged her to go and took her to live in the hospital nursing quarters thinking she would have a better life.

Grace was so sad the day they left Constance in Guernsey, watching the island fade away when the ferry boat was returning to Poole harbour. Of course, that was a few years ago.

Back to life with Stephen . . .

After a while he got a job as a cleaner at a big hotel with a bar on the seafront. He cleaned the bar. It seems the bar manager left and as Stephen was full of confidence and chatty, he said to the hotel manager, "I could do that job," and applied for the job.

Well, to his surprise he got the job as bar manager. He loved the job and, after about 6 months he got a job for Grace as a barmaid. It was busy and long hours, starting at 11am until 3pm, home for lunch then back at 6.30pm to look after the bar. Working until 11pm when the bar closed but cleaning up the bar and all the staff had a drink together until 12-12.30am, home by 1am. This went on for 4 years. They were kept very busy.

After 1 year together, Stephen bought a car from a neighbour who was selling it cheap. They called the car 'Crasselda'. So, they had wheels and went out in the country every minute they could, £5 of petrol lasting a week for them. Life was looking up for the couple. Stephen loved his job as manager, talking to customers and drinking a drink but Grace worked hard collecting glasses, serving customers and putting glasses in the glass washer and keeping the bar clean. As it happened, Grace wasn't so happy, long, busy hours, serving bar lunches at lunchtime, no home life really. She still had to clean the house and make meals. She had one day off a week, on a Monday. It really was a busy bar.

One night a week they started to put a jazz band on or an artiste singing. That brought more customers in and the bar was very busy. At weekends sometimes, coaches of people came into the bar, all arranged by the couple.

The happiest times were when they went for rides into the country, Bleasdale Fells, Garstang, walking along canal towpaths. They loved the outdoor life and walked miles and ate out at different venues. Such a good time . . . but dark clouds are starting to form in Grace's life . . .

As everyone knows, reader, good things never last forever.

On a Monday night Grace had a night off from work so Stephen was away from Grace and worked but he started staying out all night and not coming home. At midnight Grace would ring the hotel up and enquire where Stephen was and had he left? Grace hated doing that but anything could have happened, a car crash, anything. As she was so insecure through previous events in her life, she really suffered emotionally. She couldn't sleep, waiting for the key in the door and him coming home. It was so hurtful.

It seems there was a cocktail bar open all night so he preferred that to coming home! He would come home in the early hours and Grace would cook him egg and bacon, etc. It's amazing what love does to a person! Forgive anything but trust soon was lost. They still carried on a usual, playing music, Level 42 one of their favourites, going out in the car and enjoying their time together. Kate Bush, a favourite of Grace's.

Now, some customers used to say to Grace, "Why don't you get a place of your own? A little pub in the country?" and a seed was born in their minds. Yes, that would be lovely, no travelling backwards and forwards, living on the job and just going downstairs to work.

So, a new phase starts in the couple's life. It takes 2 years travelling around the country looking for a little pub with business that they could afford. 2 years going to Wales, all over England but really, they couldn't afford many places. Then, one day, they visit a little country pub called 'The Blue Bell' and fall in love with it.

All the forms are signed and Grace's house up for sale. All belongings, possessions put into boxes and a problem turns up. It seems the plumbing isn't right and a septic tank runs into a field so the place, the pub, is closed down. So, hunting starts again for a suitable place.

6 months later a little country pub looks good, takings good, karaoke being the draw to the country customers. Still a problem with finance. The people in the little pub are desperate to move out and move to the city so they have an idea to help Grace and Stephen out. Do a swap, which they do, the house for the pub. The worst thing that Grace has ever done but, being so eager to move on with her life and better herself, it seems very exciting!

So, the day arrives to move. The lorry arrives to take Grace's furniture and belongings and they follow the furniture lorry in their car, full of excitement and foreboding. Alison was so sad to be leaving the family home but time had moved on – but fancy leaving this lovely home and long garden!

They had said their goodbyes to all friends and workmates. A really big move in their lives!

When they arrived at their new home the fire alarm was going off and, try as they could, they couldn't turn it off. It was making such a loud noise and so embarrassing for the couple. Anyway, after a few phone calls someone came out to stop this outside alarm but there weren't any customers! The searches by the solicitor had taken so long the other owners of the pub had run the pub down. It was such a shock for the couple.

After a time, people started to come in, more through curiosity than anything and business looked up. Hard work, mind you, but Stephen was a good host and had the 'gift of the gab'.

2-3 years went by and trade started to fall off, not

much money being taken really because of VAT, business tax, entertainment tax if you have a jukebox, no money for our couple, only long hours and hard work. A little food was done.

Then, one day, it seems a customer, a local, buys a rundown pub in the next village and does it up and opens it up. All their customers decided to support this milkman's pub in the next village and some think they can go to our couple's pub at 10pm for last drinks. Takings are down, can't pay the mortgage, the bank sends 3 letters, £30 each letter, charged to them, to tell them they have £6.99 short in the bank.

Well, that starts the ball rolling for disaster. Missing on payments of mortgage and one can't catch up with so little takings. Grace loved the pub with its beams and history, a 100-year-old building. She felt like Lorna Doone when it snowed and she walked up the hill outside, in the snow, during the Winter but didn't really like the life – the late nights, long hours, nothing but worry about money and debt.

After 4 years they had to close down and move out, all dreams shattered and lost. Disgrace for Grace for forfeiting her lovely home for this broken dream. They moved out and got a cottage in a nearby village belonging to the council. Grace loved the cottage: 2 bedrooms with a small parlour and very large kitchen. Stephen decorated it and sorted the garden out which was long and full of brambles. The cottage was one of 4 which used to be a blacksmith's a 100 years previous and was made into 4 cottages. It was lovely but Grace felt so depressed, no friends and family miles away and she was so unhappy.

By this time Alison had two sons, lovely little boys and Grace had bought some bunkbeds for when they came to stay on holiday. There was Sam, the Siamese cat, who was very lovely and verbal. The cat had been at the pub also for the 4 years they were.

It was lovely where the cottage was, trees, flowers everywhere but Grace wasn't perfectly happy. Stephen started going home to his family, not giving Grace any phone number to get in touch with him. It seemed so strange. No jobs for either of them, living on benefits, rent collector used to call every week for the rent. Grace couldn't forgive Stephen for his behaviour in the pub, drinking too much of the profits, smoking too much, buying cigs from the machine, losing money, smoking behind the bar and all the insecurity he'd given her! She starts to resent him, all love gone!

So, one day, he said he's going to see family up north so she says, "Stay there then!" So, she gives him lots of thing he would need in a flat, pressure cooker, towels, etc and off he goes. The end of another chapter lasting ten years.

Now I must say, reader, that it sounds a very sad ten years but it was and it wasn't.

The couple had done so many nice things together which is so nice for Grace. She had been married 30 years to Robbo and never been out together as Robbo was always working away as a bus driver and HGV driver so it was so new to Grace to do such a lot of things together with Stephen; going on long walks together, eating in restaurants, living life to the full, just as it should be.

Grace looked nice, her best in her life. She dressed up, felt good and young. The most wonderful things they did, arranged by Grace, was have weekends away in the Lake District all before she took on the village pub. They had a holiday in Sicily and Egypt, stayed at the 'Luxor Hilton Hotel', just like a hotel off a James Bond film set.

Grace used to save up best she could and pay with her credit card and pay it off after the holiday. They went to the 'Valley of the Kings', so hot! Into Tutankhamun's tomb and many more, something Grace always wanted to see.

In Sicily they were always looking for the Mafia, making signs with their fingers. All such wonderful holidays, Grace closing her eyes to early behaviour by Stephen.

The holidays were taken in 1988. It wouldn't be safe now to do the things they did and saw in and 1980s but pressure from the pub, hard work, shortage of money, love flew out of the window. So sad but that's life!

Another chapter starting in Grace's life . . .

Well, reader, I've come to the last chapter. 20 years have flown by. I'm in my 80s now, my eyesight is fading and I feel I must finish what I started 83 years ago.

Grace is keeping well, she spent 4 years in the 2-bedroomed cottage she had with her Siamese cat called Sam but, unfortunately, he was 13 years old which is a good age for a pedigree cat. He had to be put to sleep because his kidneys and internal organs were shutting down. The vet kept warning her about his health deteriorating but she didn't want to have him put to sleep and looked after him like a baby, carrying him to his tray, etc. The vet gave him an injection and it seems, overnight, the cat had a heart attack or something. He kept turning around in circles in the morning so she had to give in and had him put to sleep. Grace was heartbroken.

She wrote poetry and she wrote two poems about Sam and had them published. 6 poems were published altogether. It seems when a person is emotional, sad, they can write poetry.

Grace loved the cottage and garden but missed her family so decided to move nearer to Alison and the boys. She got a 1-bedroom bungalow for elderly people, 5 years waiting to hear from the council. All the possessions, plants also moved to the new address. A lot of stress for Grace.

So, life goes into routine. She gets another cat from a neighbour's friend who had some feral cats coming into the place where she worked and felt the mother cat wouldn't last the Winter, living the life it had. So, Grace felt sorry and took the beautiful black, feral cat in to live with her. It was so scared it climbed up the curtains in the kitchen and stayed on the top of the kitchen cupboards for weeks to feel safe and come into the lounge.

Well, this cat is still living with Grace and has turned into her best friend and company. The cat she called 'Lucky' because she was living with Grace and spoiled, never strayed, stayed on the patio in the back garden so Grace felt secure with her. It's a little female cat with a little white at the end of her tail.

Alison lives nearby and they go out to garden centres for lunch, sitting in the sun and enjoying the pleasure. Alison has grown very close to Grace and is her best friend. She drives so she takes Grace out, to the theatre, sometimes shopping together, etc. The two lovely sons, boys, are men now and come around to see Grace often. And Grace is very lucky as she goes on holiday twice a year and loves it. It gives her something to look forward to. She goes on her own with a coach firm and travels all over the world. Sun, sea, nice clothes you don't wear at home and dress up for dinner for the meal at night in the hotel.

She has never bothered with men as she doesn't trust them after her experiences earlier in her life. She doesn't miss the company; she has her family and Lucky. They go out for lovely meals on birthdays and life is good. Grace loves antique programmes and some television programmes. Life is slowing down. She loves her garden and has green fingers so everything looks lovely, a great pleasure of our heroine.

So, I'll close this story now and say bye now and God Bless for reading this story of Grace.

**Dawn – My Lament**

In the stillness of the night
Not a car or bus in sight
In the quiet of the street
Not a single soul to meet.

In the loneliness of my room
Morning, it can't come too soon
First, it's three and then it's six
Oh, how loudly that clock ticks.

Laying on my rumpled bed
Why do things keep going through my head?
How loud my heart does pound
When will morning come around?

I get up and look out
And see nature's wonders all about
The trees and shrubs, oh so green
Oh, isn't it a lovely scene?

Loneliness is so profound
I wait upon every sound
Long, yes, how I long
To hear the blackbird's lovely song.

The robin and the sparrow too
To bring me nearer to you
Also longing for my feline friend
And bring this night to an end.

Oh, lover, where have you been?
You can make my heart scream
I've just heard your key in the door
No more loneliness anymore.

## Holidays started in 1976 aged 40

| 1976 | Isle of Elba – Florence |
| 1977 | Tenerife |
| 1978 | Athens, Greece |
| 1979 | Israel |
| 1988 | Egypt |
| 1989 | Sicily |
| 1986 | Menorca (twice) |
| 1990 | Jersey (4 times, Spain |
|      | Guernsey twice |
| 1991 | Malta |
| 1975 | Edinburgh |
|      | London 4 times |

| | |
|---|---|
| 1976/2006 | Paris |
| 2005 | Portugal (twice) |
| 2006 | Venice and Verona and Lake Garda |
| 2007 | Sorrento and Pompeii and Herculaneum |
| 2010 | Lake Como |
| 2011-12 | Spain, Roses |
| 2013 | Majorca, Spain |
| 2014 | Lido-de-Jessilow |
| 2015 | Scotland |
| 2015 | Menorca, Spain |
| 2015 | Jessilow, Spain |
| 2011 | Guernsey |
| 2015 | Torquay, Scotland |
| 2016 | Torquay, Ireland, Jersey, Normandy Beaches Blackpool |
| 2017 | Cornwall |
| 2017 | Croatia, Italy, Dolomites |
| 2017 | Blackpool |
| 2018 | Andorra, Blackpool |
| 2018 | Denia, Spain |

**Sam, My Feline Friend**
Oh Sam, Sam, where are you?
I hope you are happy in the sky so blue
Your warmth, your loud mew
If only you knew how I miss you
My lonely heart cries out for you
Why, oh why do I feel so blue?
How can I start anew?

Why do I grieve so much?
Because I miss your gentle touch
The pain I feel cries to get out
Oh, why can't I cry and shout
When I feel like crying my heart out?

Oh, Sam, why, oh why
Did you have to go and make me cry?
You were the apple of my eye
I hope you will be happy in the great blue sky
You were such a friend, why did your life had to end?

All the hurt and pain I feel
When is it going to heal?
You were loyal to the end
My one and only true friend
Why do I grieve so much?
Maybe because I miss your gentle touch
For 12 years I had you
How will I ever start anew?

**My Friend**

My heart is like an open door
Love doesn't live here anymore
The people that I love and knew
What has happened to you?

Thomas Hardy, who I adore
Why didn't you write more?
The return of the native above all
Is simply the one I adore!
I long to come and see your tomb
Installed in that very large room.

All your heroines are so sublime
All are such friends of mine
The heroes are my friends too
Oh, I wish I could talk to you.
The hurt, the pain, that I endure
I do wish there was a cure
The sleepless nights, the loneliness
Will I be happy anymore?

You are but my only friend
Without you my life would be at an end
I could never endure the long days
And nights anymore.

How I can't wait to read your books
Again and again escape
The loneliness within my soul
And make me whole again.